The BIG Book of Camping Jokes and Riddles

By Thomas C. Mercaldo

D0106603

1

Table of Contents

Camping Lore

What do you call a small cat that puts band aids on cuts?
> *A first aid kit.*

What is the best way to start a fire with two sticks?
> *Make sure one of the sticks is a match.*

Where will campers sleep in the 25th century?
> *In the future tents.*

I know a camper who thinks he's an owl.
> *When the camper asks "Who?" answer, make that two campers that think they're owls.*

What happened to the camper who put a firecracker in the pancake batter?
> *When the pancakes came, he blew his stack.*

Why did the leader plan a parade for 3/4/2099?

He wanted the troops to March forth in the future.

Why wasn't the girl afraid when the lion escaped from the zoo?

She heard it was a man eating lion.

Did you hear the joke about the rope?

Skip it.

What did the kindling wood say to the fireplace?

Goodbye, I've met my match.

What happened to the match that lost its temper?

It flared up.

What happened to the campers that played with matches?

They made complete ashes of themselves.

What do you call a hill that campers cook their meals on?

A mountain range.

What kind of knots are tied in space?

Astro-knots.

Why did the camper salute the refrigerator?

It was a General Electric.

Did you hear about the boy who wrote an essay about his compass?
He called it his compassition.

What happened to the girl who wanted to be a piece of firewood?
She made a fuel of herself.

What do you call a boomerang that doesn't return?
A stick.

What do you call it when a student promises to be faithful to furniture polish?
Pledge Allegiance.

What do you get when you cross a baseball player with a camper?
Someone who likes to pitch tents.

7

What happened to the boy who ironed a four leaf clover?

He really pressed his luck.

Why did the insect eat on the tent flap?

It was a dining fly.

What do you get when you cross a brook and a stream?

Wet feet.

What does it mean when the barometer is falling?

Whoever nailed it up didn't do a good job.

How did the hiker feel when he came out of the woods?

Bushed.

What do they do at camp when it rains?

Let it rain.

Can you drop a full canteen without spilling any water?

Yes, if the canteen is filled with soda.

What did the father buffalo say to his son when he was leaving camp?
Bye Son (Bison).

How do you make a fire lighter?
Take off one log.

What do you call it when you bring the king camping and he climbs a mountain?
HiKing.

How do you avoid getting sick from insect bites while camping?
Don't bite any insects.

What did the boy do with the tree after he chopped it down?
He chopped it up.

If there is a kidnapping at camp what should you do?
Wake him up.

What does it mean when you find a horseshoe at camp?
Some poor horse is going around barefoot.

Why did the campers invite Mariano Rivera to go camping?
They needed someone to pitch the tents.

Where do backpackers keep their sleeping bags?
In their nap sacks (Knapsacks).

Where is it best to find books about the trees at camp?
A branch Library.

How do you make a hot dog stand in the middle of the woods?
Steal his chair.

Why don't elephants bring backpacks to camp?
They keep everything in their trunks.

Why did the ghost stop scaring the campers at camp?
His haunting license expired.

Why were all the baby ants at camp confused?
Because all of their uncles were ants.

Does camp have both hot and cold water?
Yes. Cold in the winter, and hot in the summer.

What insect sits in a circle of rocks blinking its tail light?
A Camp Fire Fly.

What did the Quarterback say to the kids at camp?
Hike.

At camp, what rises in the morning and waves all day?
The American Flag.

Why can't the mountain climber ever improve?

Because he's reached his peak.

Why did Joe Camper cook beef in his tent?

He wanted tent steaks.

What happened to the Camper who refinished the wooden flagpole?

He varnished into thin air.

You go camping and you only have one match. On arriving at the cabin you find a wood burning stove in one corner, a kerosene lantern in another corner and a candle in the third corner. What would you light first?

The match.

What do you get when you cross poison ivy and a four leaf clover?

A rash of good luck.

What do you call a small canvas doghouse?

A pup tent.

What's the best way to carve wood?

Whittle by whittle.

Why shouldn't the kids at camp swim on an empty stomach?

Because it's easier to swim on water.

The Wild Adirondack Cow

For those who do not live in the Northeast, this section requires a special introduction. The Wild Adirondack Cow is a carnivorous moose-like creature that inhabited the Adirondack and Berkshire valleys. Similar to a Holstein in shape and color, the much larger Wild Adirondack Cow features a wide jaw and bear-like teeth. Most scientists believe the Wild Adirondack Cow (WAC) is now extinct, nonetheless, many campers claim to have seen the creature in recent times. Tales about this vicious relative of the grizzly bear are a central theme in Indian folklore.

After much effort the Indians developed a method of making wool out of Wild Adirondack Cow's milk.
> Unfortunately, it made the cows feel a little sheepish.

Did you hear about the Wild Adirondack Cow that ate bits of metal every night?

It was his staple diet.

A Wild Adirondack Cow went to see the eye doctor because he kept bumping into things.

"You need glasses," said the doctor.
"Will I be able to read with them?"
"Yes," the doctor replied.
"That's great," replied the Wild Adirondack Cow. "I always wished I could read."

"I thought I told you to draw a picture of a Wild Adirondack Cow eating grass," said the art counselor. "Why have you handed in a blank sheet of paper?"

"Because the cow ate all the grass, that's why there's no grass."

16

"But what about the Wild Adirondack Cow?"
"There wasn't much point in him hanging around when there was nothing to eat so he left."

"Why are you tearing up your handbook and scattering it around the camp?" the furious leader asked."
"To keep Wild Adirondack Cows away."
"There are no Wild Adirondack Cows at this camp," snapped the Leader."
"Shows how effective it is, doesn't it?"

Three animals were sitting in the forest debating over which was the most feared. The first, a hawk, claimed animals feared him because he could repeatedly attack undetected from above. The second animal, a lion, said he was king of the feared animals because he possessed superior speed and strength. The skunk insisted he was feared above the others because he could frighten away animals without needing flight, nor strength. As the group argued, A Wild Adirondack Cow appeared, and proved he was the most feared animal that ever lived.

Before they could utter another word, he ate them all - hawk, lion and stinker.

Did you hear that revolutionary war soldiers sent a group of Wild Adirondack Cows into space to orbit the earth?

Apparently, it was the herd shot round the world.

Why shouldn't you cry if a Wild Adirondack Cow falls on the ice?

Because there is no use crying over spilled milk.

What happens to a Wild Adirondack Cow when it stands out in the rain?

It gets wet.

Where can you find Wild Adirondack Cow artifacts?

In a Moo-seum.

Were Wild Adirondack Cow cannibalistic?
Yes, many were known to eat their fodder.

Do you know how long Wild Adirondack Cows should be milked?
The same as short Wild Adirondack Cows.

What would you get if you feed a Wild Adirondack Cow $100 dollar bills?
You'd get rich milk.

Why shouldn't you cry over spilled milk?
It will get too salty.

Why was the Wild Adirondack Cow afraid?
Because he was a Cow-ard.

Why did the Indians place bells on Wild Adirondack Cows?
Because their horns don't work.

What do you call a Wild Adirondack Cow with no ears?

> *Whatever you want; he can't hear you.*

What did the Eskimos call the northern relative of the Wild Adirondack Cow?

> *The Wild Eski-MOO's.*

Where did the Wild Adirondack Cow go when he lost his tail?

> *To a retail store.*

What made the Wild Adirondack Cow's dreams come true?

> *His dairy God-mother.*

What do you call a Wild Adirondack Cow that can't give milk?

> *An udder failure.*

What did one Wild Adirondack Cow say to the other?

> *Nothing, Wild Adirondack Cows can't talk.*

How do you keep a Wild Adirondack Cow from charging?

Take away his credit card.

Where does a Wild Adirondack Cow go for entertainment?

To the mooovies.

When do Wild Adirondack Cows blow their horns?

When they're stuck in traffic.

What do you call Wild Adirondack Cows that ride on trains?

Passengers.

What does See O double you stand for?

Cow.

What did the Wild Adirondack Cow say
after eating a DVD?
> *I liked the book better.*

What is black and white and blue all over?
> *A Wild Adirondack Cow at the North
> Pole.*

What would you call it if a Wild
Adirondack Cow helped perform surgery?
> *Cow-operation.*

What do Wild Adirondack Cows have that
no other animal has?
> *Wild Adirondack Calves.*

What is black and white and blue and
hides in caves?
> *A Wild Adirondack Cow that's afraid
> of polar bears.*

What do you call a Wild Adirondack Cow at the North Pole?

Lost.

What is black and white, black and white, black and white, and yellow?

Three Wild Adirondack Cows eating a banana.

What is black and white and red all over?

A newspaper.

Why can't you teach a Wild Adirondack Cow to dance?

Because it has two left feet.

Why did the astronauts find bones on the moon?

The first cow didn't make it.

What happens to Wild Adirondack Cows that stay in the pasture all night?

They get pasteurized.

Why don't many Wild Adirondack Cows go to college?

Because not many graduate from high school.

Why does a WAC kneel before it attacks?

Because it is preying.

A Wild Adirondack Cow is tied to a rope 8 feet long. A bale of hay is 24 feet 5 inches away, and the Wild Adirondack Cow wants to eat the hay. How can he do it?

He can just walk over and eat it. The rope isn't tied to anything.

What kind of sandwiches do female Wild Adirondack Cows like?

Bull-only.

What type of coffee do mother WAC's drink?

De-calf-inated.

What do you call a sleeping male WAC?
A bull-dozer.

Why did the Wild Adirondack Cow say,
"Baa, baa?"
*He was trying to learn a second
language.*

How do you make a Wild Adirondack
Cow stew?
Leave him waiting for 5 or 6 hours.

Why did the Wild Adirondack Cow cross
the road?
It was the chicken's day off.

Why did the Wild Adirondack Cow cross
the highway?
To prove he wasn't chicken.

What's black and white and green?
A seasick Wild Adirondack Cow.

What's black and white and blue?
An extremely sad Wild Adirondack Cow.

What Cow baseball player holds the most milk?
The pitcher.

What's black and white and black and blue?
A Wild Adirondack Cow that fell down a hill.

What do you say to a Wild Adirondack Cow that gets in your way?
MOOOve over.

Why did the Wild Adirondack Cow
change his socks on the golf course?
He got a hole in one.

Wild Adirondack Cow with large black
spots married a Wild Adirondack Cow
with small black spots. Their first son had
no spots. What did they call him?
Harold.

Where do young Wild Adirondack Cows
eat lunch?
In a calf-ateria.

Where do you find Wild Adirondack Cows
that are waiting to get into the game?
In the bull-pen.

What did the Wild Adirondack Cow wear
on his head during the baseball game?
A baseball cap.

Wild Adirondack Cow Attack Survival Guide.

1. Use the buddy system. If a Wild Adirondack cow attacks, push your buddy toward the cow.
2. Hold up a large mirror to the WAC, he'll think he's being attacked.
3. Carry a 50 gallon milking machine with you at all times.
4. Stay out of the woods.

Some speakers at campfires are like male Wild Adirondack cows. A point here, a point there, and a lot of bull in between.

Indian Lore

Why did the Indian wear feathers in his hair?
To keep his wig warm.

What do the Indians call a twisted path through their corn fields?
A maize.

What three letters does Chief Sequassen use to signify his heritage?
N D N. (Indian)

What did they call Chief Sequassen's single daughter when she got in trouble?
Mischief.

What did Chief Sequassen call the ranger
when he got his head caught in a bucket?
>*Pail face.*

What's an Indian forum?
>*Two-um plus two-um.*

Did the local Indians hunt bear?
>*Not when it was cold out.*

What did the local Indians call 5 frogs
stacked on top of each other?
>*A toad-em pole.*

Chief Sequassen

A turtle went to see Chief Sequassen. "I'm terribly shy," the turtle confessed to the wise old chief. "Can you cure me?"

"Absolutely," said Chief Sequassen. "I'll have you out of your shell in no time."

Many moons ago Chief Sequassen traveled to visit a tribe on the eastern shore of Lake Michigan. Shortly after he arrived, a huge pillar of smoke came billowing across the lake.

"Oh wise Chief Sequassen," a young brave asked, "can you explain the meaning of this smoke signal?"
The Old Chief studied it for a moment and then replied, "I've not often seen signals in this dialect, but apparently it says a Mrs. O'Leary has had some trouble with her cow."

A group of Indian chiefs had gathered and were sitting around the campfire telling stories. "We have a young brave in our tribe," one chief said who never forgets anything. "The devil can have my soul if I'm not telling the truth."

Later that night the devil visited the Indian Chief. "Come along with me and let's find out if I'm going to get your soul." They went together to visit the young brave. "Do you like eggs?" the devil inquired of the brave.

"Yes," the young Indian responded. The devil was poised to ask another question when a legion of goblins called him away on other business. Twenty-five years later, the old chief died, and the devil dashed off in search of the brave.

"How," said the devil, his right arm raised in Indian fashion.

"Over-easy," replied the brave.

Once there was an Indian whose name was Shortcake. He lived with his wife, Squaw. Sadly, Shortcake died. Chief Sequassen wandered over to Squaw to see what she would do with the dead body.

She relied, "Squaw bury Shortcake."

A builder decided to clear a wooded area in order to build a new golf course. Shortly after the project started Chief Sequassen, who lived nearby, wandered up to the foreman and said, "Rain tomorrow."

Sure enough, the next day it rained. A week later Chief Sequassen again visited the workman and said, "Storm tomorrow."
The following day there was an incredible hailstorm.
The foreman said to his assistant. "That Indian is incredible. When we lay down the greens we will need 3 consecutive days of nice weather. You'd better hire that Indian to tell us when we can lay the greens."
Chief Sequassen successfully predicted several more storms, but then unexpectedly, stopped coming by. The foreman was anxious to lay

the final greens so he sent for Chief Sequassen.

When the Chief finally came, the foreman began. "I rely on your wisdom," the foreman stated. "What will the weather be like tomorrow?" Chief Sequassen shrugged and said, "I don't know, my radio is broken."

A pilot was flying over Chief Sequassen's reservation when he began having trouble with his engine.

Thinking fast he put on his parachute and bailed out of the plane,
floating gently to the ground.
Unfortunately, he landed right in the Old Chief's cooking pot,
which was simmering gently over a fire.
The surprised chief looked at the pilot and asked, "What's this flier doing in my soup?"

Chief Sequassen was sending smoke signals, when suddenly he put aside his regular blanket and began using a baby blanket.

"What's that for?" a bystander asked.

"I'm making small talk," Chief Sequassen responded.

Chief Sequassen was riding his horse on the open prairie when he stumbled upon an Indian with his ear to the ground. Chief Sequassen got down from his horse and put his ear to the ground. After a few minutes he spoke. "I don't hear anything," the Chief stated.

"I know," the Indian replied, "It's been like this all day.

Trader Jack

Why did the workers at the U.S. mint go on strike?

They wanted to make less money.

What do you get when you cross a lemon with a cat?

A sour puss.

When it came time to migrate north, two elderly vultures doubted they had the energy to make the trip so they decided to go by plane. When they checked their baggage, the attendant noticed they were carrying two dead armadillos.

"Do you want to check the armadillos as luggage?" he asked.
"No thanks," the vultures replied.
"They're carrion".

Two farmers were discussing their cattle. One inquired, "What did you give your bull last year when it was sick?"

"Fed him kerosene," the farmer responded. They then went on their separate ways.

Months later, the farmers met again. The first farmer said, "Say Jake, you told me you fed your bull kerosene when he was sick. I gave that to mine and he died."

"Yep," Jake responded, "killed mine too."

A bus carrying all the local congressmen was speeding down a country road. After passing a small farmhouse, the bus swerved into a field and hit a huge oak tree. A farmer ran out of the farmhouse to investigate the crash. Then he dug a hole and buried all the politicians. A few days later, the local sheriff drove by in search of the missing congressmen, and he saw the damaged bus. He got the farmer, and asked him what happened to all the politicians.

The farmer said, "I buried them."

The surprised sheriff wondered, "Were they all dead?"

The farmer replied, "Some of them were trying to tell me they weren't, but you know how politicians lie"

Did you hear about the ship bound for New York filled with yo-yos that got caught in a violent storm?
It sank 25 times.

What happened to the man who fell into the lens grinding machine?
He made a spectacle of himself.

Did you hear about the cross-eyed teacher?
She could not control her pupils.

The newly hired musician was having trouble keeping the beat with the ship's orchestra. The captain grew annoyed and finally threatened the new musician.

> "Either you learn to keep time or I'll throw you overboard. It's up to you; sync or swim."

What happened to the dentist who married a manicurist?
They fought tooth and nail.

Once there was a boy whose parents named him Odd. Throughout his life, everyone teased him about his name. As he grew old, he wrote out his final wishes. "I've been the butt of jokes all my life," he said. "I don't want people making fun of me after I'm gone." He asked to be buried in the middle of the wilderness with a tombstone that does not bear his name.

> After his death, people stumbled upon the large blank stone and said, "That's odd."

An American Camper visited Great Britain. He entered the lobby of a hotel and pushed the button to call the elevator.

After a lengthy wait, he grew impatient and asked, "Why is there such a delay?"

The hotel clerk responded, "Be patient, the lift will be down directly."

"The lift?" replied the American Camper. "Oh, you mean the elevator."

"No, I mean the lift," replied the Englishman, annoyed by the American's arrogant attitude.

"I think I should know what it is called," said the American. "After all, elevators were invented in the United States."

"Perhaps," retorted the Englishman. "But the language was invented here."

Two goats were snooping around the back of a video rental store when they came upon a discarded DVD. One goat hungrily devoured the tape. His companion watched him and, when he had finished asked, "How was it?"

The first goat replied, "Frankly, the book was better."

How many jellybeans can you put in an empty jar?

One, after that the jars no longer empty.

An Atheist was walking through a very desolate part of the northern forest. Suddenly, he heard a ferocious howl as Big Foot sprung onto the path directly to his rear. The creature picked him up and hurled him to the ground. The Atheist got up and began to run with all his might in an attempt to escape the attacking creature. As the Big Foot once again drew near, the atheist cried out, "Oh God, help me, save me."

At once the skies opened and the brutal attack scene froze in place with Big Foot hairy arms and dangerous claws just inches away from the Atheist. A booming voice came from the sky, "I thought you didn't believe in me."

"Oh please, God, give me a break," the man pleaded.

"Up until 10 minutes ago, I didn't believe in Big Foot either."

Did you hear about the new restaurant on the moon?

> *The food is great but there's no atmosphere.*

"Tell me," the priest asked a cannibal. "Do you think religion has made any progress here?"

> "Absolutely," the native replied. "Now we only eat fisherman on Fridays."

A Kansas farmer died and left his entire estate to his only son. Twenty-four hours later, the bank foreclosed on the farm.

"Well," stammered the son, "Dad did say that the farm would be mine one day."

What lies at the bottom of the ocean and quivers?

A nervous wreck.

Why didn't the cannibal eat the clown?

He tasted funny.

Long ago Chief Sequassen was about to die so he called for Rugged Mountain and Falling Rocks, the two bravest warriors of the tribe. The Old Chief instructed each to go out and seek buffalo skins. Whoever returned with the most skins would be the chief. About a month later Rugged Mountain returned with one hundred pelts, but Falling Rocks never returned.

Even today as you drive down the highways that pass through the old tribal territory you can see signs that say: Watch out for Falling Rocks.

What school did Sherlock Holmes graduate from?

Elementary, my dear Watson.

How do you spell blind pig?

B-L-N-D P-G. A blind pig doesn't have any eyes.

Three elderly sisters had lived together all their lives and they were getting very forgetful.

One went upstairs to take a bath. She filled the tub, stepped in with one foot and said, "Was I getting into the tub or getting out?
I'll have to ask my sister."
She called for her sister and asked, "Was I getting into the tub or getting out?"
The sister replied, "I don't know, I'll come upstairs and look!"
As she started to go upstairs, she said, "Was I going up the stairs or coming down? I'll have to ask my sister.

45

Was I going up the stairs or down the stairs," she inquired of sister number three.

"I don't know," she replied.

"Thank goodness I'm not forgetful like my other two sisters, she said as she knocked on wood."

Was that the front door or the back door?"

What do you call a deer with no eyes?
No eye deer (no idea).

A young brave walked up to Chief Sequassen while he was sending smoke signals. The brave wondered aloud. How come you have two campfires, a large and a small one?

> I use the small one for local calls,
> and the big one for long distance.

A doctor tells his patient, "I've got some good news and some bad news for you."

> So the patient asks, "What's the good news Doc?"
> And the doctor says, "They're going to name a disease after you."

A waiter in a large restaurant was stricken and rushed to a nearby hospital's emergency room. On the operating table and in great pain, he waited for attention. An intern who had recently been to the restaurant passed by. The patient pleaded, "Help me, Doc, "Can't you do something?"

> "I'm sorry," the intern retorted.
> "This isn't my table."

The Camp Ranger

The camp ranger was walking through a desolate side of camp when he caught wind of something burning in the distance. Farther along the trail he found an elderly hermit cooking a meal.

"What's cooking?" the ranger asked.

"Peregrine Falcon," replied the hermit.

"Peregrine Falcon!" the ranger exclaimed. "Don't you know they are an endangered species, and that it is illegal to eat them?"

"I'm sorry," the hermit said, "but I've had no contact with the outside world in more than 30 years. How could I have known?"

The ranger agreed not to report the old timer this time, but made him promise never to eat falcon again. As he was leaving, curiosity got the best of the old ranger and he asked, "What does Peregrine Falcon taste like anyway?"

"Well", replied the hermit, "it's sort of a cross between bald eagle and whooping crane."

What happened to the skydiver whose parachute didn't open?
He jumped to a conclusion.

After several failed attempts at conventional fishing Joe Camper endeavored to improve his luck. So he went out on the lake and began dropping sticks of dynamite over the side. He waited for the boom and began scooping the fish out with a net.

After he'd done this 3 or 4 times the camp ranger rushed over and said, "Joe, you know you aren't allowed to fish like that."
Joe Camper paid him little attention. Lighting up another stick of dynamite he handed it to the ranger and said, "you gonna talk, or are you gonna fish?"

"The sign says no fishing allowed," the ranger said as Joe Camper cast out his line.
"I saw the sign," Joe Camper responded, "so I'm fishing silently."

What do you say when the Statue of Liberty sneezes?
God Bless America.

What do you call a cloistered priest eating potato chips?
A chip monk.

The ranger was out chopping down a dead tree when a short thin man walked by.

"That's not the way to chop down a tree," the little guy yelled.

"Oh no," responded the surprised camp ranger.

He handed the ax to the other man. "Suppose you show me how it's done."

With one swing of the ax, the little guy brought the tree crashing to the ground.

"That's amazing," the ranger stammered. "Where did you ever learn to do that?"

"I used to be a lumberjack in the Sahara forest," the little stranger answered.

"What do you mean the Sahara forest," replied the ranger. "It's the Sahara desert."

"It is now."

What do people in Canada call little black cats?

Kittens.

The ranger took a group of boys from camp on a white water rafting trip.

"Don't be alarmed," he told the Campers, "I know every rock in the river."

Just then, the boat overturned and flipped them all into the river.

"See," said the ranger, "there's one now."

The ranger found Joe Camper fishing in the lake right next to a sign that said, "No fishing allowed."

"What's the meaning of this Joe?" the ranger asked?

"Oh I'm not fishing," Joe replied. "I'm just teaching these worms to swim."

What happened when a ship carrying red paint collided with a ship carrying purple paint?

Both crews were marooned.

What's the best way to get rid of evil spirits?

Exorcise a lot.

Where were the first french fries made?

In Grease.

How many apples grow on a tree?

All of them.

A visitor to camp asked the ranger what time it was. The ranger quickly responded that he thought it was about 12 o'clock.

The surprised visitor wondered, "Only 12 o'clock, I thought it was much later than that."

"Oh, it never gets later than 12

at this camp," the ranger responded.
"How can that be?" the puzzled
visitor queried.
"Well, after 12:00," the ranger
replied, "it goes back to one again."

Why do some people press the elevator
button with their thumb and other people
press it with their forefinger?
To signal for the elevator.

What happened to the thief that stole a
calendar?
He got 12 months.

How do you make soup golden?
Just add 24 carrots.

Joe Camper was walking by a camp phone
when it began to ring. He answered it, and
went straight to get the ranger. "I think
you're wanted on the phone, sir," Joe said
to the ranger.
"What do you mean, think?"
the ranger asked.

"Well," Joe stuttered, "when I answered the phone the voice on the other end said, "Is that you, you old fool?"

The beaver patrol entered the camp after traveling through a remote and rather uninteresting portion of the state. Noticing a "scenic route" sign, the Campers got into a discussion about whether it would be better to take the longer scenic route, or whether they should continue down the rather uninteresting route they had been traveling. They approached the ranger with the question, "What will we see on the scenic route that we haven't seen so far"
> The ranger asked, "What have you seen so far?"
> "Nothing," replied the Campers.
> "Then you've seen most of it already," the ranger responded.

What happened to the cat that ate the ball of yarn?
> *It had mittens.*

What's the funniest animal in the world?
A stand up chameleon.

"Did anyone lose a roll of money with a
rubber band around it," the ranger asked
the campers.

      Several Campers eagerly yelled,
"I did I did."
      "Well I just found the rubber band,"
the ranger replied.

What small blood sucking insect lives on
the moon?
      A lunatic.

If there were 10 cats on a xerox machine
and one jumped off how many would be
left?
      None they were all copycats.

Joe Camper was hiking through the woods with the ranger when they came upon a couple of penguins.

"They should be taken to the zoo," the ranger said. Joe Camper agreed, and he and the two penguins left. The next day the ranger saw Joe Camper and the penguins together. "You were supposed to take them to the zoo," the ranger stated.

"I did," replied Joe Camper. "And tonight I'm taking them to the movies."

What do liars do when they die?
Lie still.

Do you say 6 plus 7 is eleven or 6 plus 7 are 11?
Neither, you say 6 plus 7 equals 13.

Joe Camper was again fishing, close to the ranger's watchful eye. He landed a very large trout and gingerly returned it to the lake. Next he caught a pickerel, but he threw that back too. After that he reeled in a little tiny bass, and with a smile, he placed the little bass on his stringer.

The ranger was confused. "Why did you keep that tiny fish after returning the others?"

Joe Camper answered, "Because I only brought my small frying pan to camp."

What is 5Q + 5Q?

When someone responds 10Q – say your welcome.

Who won the race between the cheetah and the gazelle?

The gazelle won because cheetahs never win.

The Ranger was walking through camp when he spotted Chief Sequassen banging a stick against a hollow log.

"What are you doing," the ranger inquired?

"Calling log distance", the Chief answered.

What do Alexander the Great and Smokey the Bear have in common?

The same middle name.

Where can you go that it is so quiet you can hear a pin drop?

A bowling alley.

What do you call a person who is born in Russia, raised in China, moves to America and dies in Winsted, CT?

Dead.

The Animals at Camp

What did the deer say when they saw the Ranger coming over the hill?

> *Here comes the Ranger coming over the hill.*

What did the deer say when he saw the Ranger coming over the hill wearing sunglasses?

> *Nothing, they didn't recognize him.*

How can you keep a fish from smelling?

> *Cut off its nose.*

Why isn't a skunk's nose 12 inches long?

> *Because then it would be a foot.*

How can you revive a rodent that falls into a lake?

> *Mouse to Mouse resuscitation.*

Why do mice have fur?

> *Otherwise they would be a little bare.*

What kind of bank account does a mouse have?

A Swiss account.

Where does a mouse go when its teeth hurt?

To a rodent-ist.

How do mice find their way to new places?

With a road-ent map.

What insect is known to say grace before its meals?

A praying mantis.

Why do the bees at the soccer field hum?

They don't know the words.

What did the duck say when he bought
lipstick?

Put it on my bill.

What did the impatient stag say to his
wife?

Hurry up deer.

Why do bees have sticky hair?

Because they have honeycombs.

What do bees do with their honey?

They cell it.

Why were the bees on strike?

*They wanted shorter hours and more
honey.*

Why are crows so noisy after they've been stung?

> *Bee Caws.*

What do you call a bee that speaks softly?

> *A mumble bee.*

How did the antelope and deer burn themselves?

> *Trying to make themselves at home on the range.*

Why did the crow look for a telephone?

> *He wanted to make a long distance caw.*

Why wouldn't the twin lobsters share their toys?

> *They were two shellfish.*

What has a yellow stomach and sucks sap from trees?

A yellow bellied sap sucker.

What is a yellow bellied sap sucker after he is four days old?

5 days old.

What do you call a bee born in May?

A maybe.

What did the beaver say to the tree?

It was nice gnawing you.

What's grey and stamps out forest fires?

Smokey the elephant.

Can skunks have babies?

No, they can only have skunks.

When birds fly in formation, why is one side of the V longer than the other?

Because one side has more birds in it.

How come only small toads can sit under toadstools?
Because there isn't mushroom.

What does a skunk do when it gets mad?
It raises a stink.

How do you stop a snake from striking?
Pay it decent wages.

Why do rats have long tails?
Because they can't remember short stories.

Why do seagulls fly over the sea?
Because if they flew over the bay they would be bagels.

What goes da-dot-croak, dot-dot-croak, da-da-dot croak?
A morse toad.

What should you do if you have 44 frogs on your back windshield?

Turn on the rear window defrogger.

What do you say to a hitchhiking frog?

Hop in.

How do snakes call each other?

Poison to poison.

How much birdseed should you get for a buck?

None. Deer don't eat birdseed.

What animals can jump higher than the tallest tree at camp?

All animals. Trees can't jump.

What is black and white and goes around and around?

A skunk in a revolving door.

In an outdoor Chapel, where does a skunk sit?

In a pew.

How do you stop a mouse from squeaking?
With a little motor oil.

Why was the mother owl worried about
her son?
*Because he didn't give a hoot about
anything.*

What animal is the best at Math?
Rabbits they multiply very rapidly

What animal eats with its tail?
*All animals. None of them can
remove their tail to eat.*

Why do ducks have webbed feet?
To stamp out forest fires.

Why do elephants have flat feet?
To stamp out burning ducks.

67

Joe Camper

What happened when Joe Camper ran behind the Ranger's car?
> *He got exhausted.*

What happened when Joe Camper wandered into the street looking for the traffic jam?
> *A big truck came by and gave him a jar.*

When Joe Camper's sister fell in a well why didn't he help her?
> *Because he couldn't be a brother and assist her at the same time.*

What did Joe Camper catch when he went ice fishing?
> *A cold.*

Why does Joe Camper sleep on top of his electric blanket?
> *He heard heat rises.*

How did Joe Camper clean the mouthpiece on his tuba?

With a tuba toothpaste.

Why did Joe Camper paint a red cross on his canteen before hiking across the desert?

He thought he should have a thirst aid kit.

Why did Joe Camper stand next to the bank vault?

He wanted to be on the safe side.

Why couldn't Joe Camper blow up his old car?

> *He kept burning himself on the exhaust pipe.*

Why did Joe Camper bring a stone into the bakery?

> *He wanted to rock and roll.*

Why did Joe Camper take all his clothes off at the laundromat?

> *The sign said remove clothes when washer stops.*

Why did Joe Camper go into the dressing room?

> *He heard he would come out a changed man.*

Why did Joe Camper sell his alarm clock?

> *It kept going off when he was asleep.*

Why did Joe Camper use nails for bait when he went fishing?

He was hoping to catch hammerhead sharks.

Why does Joe Camper write TGIF on all his shoes?

To remind him toes go in first.

Why did Joe Camper order an egg salad sandwich and a chicken salad sandwich for lunch?

He wanted to see which came first.

Why did Joe Camper stuff his sausages with pork on one side and corn on the other?

He heard it was hard to make both ends meat.

Why was Joe Camper convinced his watch was running fast?

Because it took him an hour to make minute rice.

Why did Joe Camper put his head to the grindstone?

He wanted to sharpen his wit.

Why did Joe Camper give his mother an X-ray of his heart?

He wanted to show her that his heart was in the right place.

Why did Joe Camper bring a raisin to the movies?

He couldn't find a date.

Why did Joe Camper hold a piece of bread in the air?

He wanted to propose a toast.

What happened when Joe Camper swallowed some uranium?

He got atomic ache.

What did Joe Camper do when he was being chased in a circle by 42 horses?

He got off the merry-go-round.

How did Joe Camper get sand in his shoes while tree climbing?

> *He was climbing Beech trees.*

When Joe Camper made a movie - why did he call it broken leg?

> *Because it had a big cast.*

Why did Joe Camper eat under the lamppost?

> *He wanted to have a light lunch.*

Why does Joe Camper need his whole patrol to help him make scrambled eggs?

> *One person needs to hold the pan while the others shake the stove.*

Why did Joe Camper throw the clock out the window?

> *He wanted to see time fly.*

Why did Joe Camper sleep under the oil tank?

> *He wanted to get up oily in the morning.*

Why was Joe Camper so tired on April fool's day?
He just had a March of 31 days.

Why did Joe Camper eat yeast and polish?
He wanted to rise and shine.

What happened to Joe Camper after he broke the law of gravity?
He got a suspended sentence.

Why was Joe Camper limping?
He strained himself walking through the screen door.

Why did Joe Camper buy a set of tools?
Because everyone kept telling him he had a screw loose.

Why was Joe Camper glad he wasn't born in Germany?
Because he can't speak German.

Why does Joe Camper carry a compass?
So he'll know whether he's coming or going.

What happened when Joe Camper threw himself on the floor?

He missed.

Why did Joe Camper stand on a ladder to sing the camp song?

He wanted to reach the high notes.

Why did Joe Camper stare at the orange juice container?

It said concentrate on it.

Why did Joe Camper put an ice-pack in his father's sleeping bag?

He wanted to have a cold pop.

Why did Joe Camper pour pancake batter on his electric blanket?

He wanted breakfast in bed.

Why did Joe Camper spray bug spray on his watch?

He wanted to get rid of the ticks.

What did Joe Camper act like a nut?

He wanted to catch a squirrel.

Why did Joe Camper take his pocket knife and a loaf of bread into the street?

He heard there was a traffic jam.

Why did Joe Camper lock his mother's sister out of the cabin during a snowstorm?

He wanted to make anti-freeze.

Why did Joe Camper put a sugar cube under his pillow?
He wanted to have sweet dreams.

Why did Joe Camper take hay into his tent at bedtime?
He wanted to feed his nightmares.

Why did Joe Camper empty his canteen?
He wanted to see a waterfall.

Why was Joe Camper glad he wasn't an eagle?
He couldn't fly.

Why did Joe Camper sit on his watch?
He wanted to be on time for the meeting.

Why did Joe Camper tiptoe past his tent?
>*He didn't want to wake up the
>sleeping bags.*

What did Joe Camper take out his pocketknife and slice his toe?
>*He was running late and wanted to make a shortcut.*

How did Joe Camper break his leg raking leaves?
>*He fell out of the tree.*

Why did Joe Camper throw a stick of butter in the air?
>*He wanted to see a butterfly.*

What did Joe Camper say when he wore a hole through his socks?
>*Darn them.*

Why did Joe Camper cut a hole in his umbrella?
>*He wanted to see when the rain
>stopped.*

Why did Joe Camper put his head on the piano?

He wanted to play it by ear.

Why did Joe Camper tie a flashlight to his bed?

Because he was a light sleeper.

Why did Joe Camper put his radio in the freezer?

He wanted to hear cool music.

Why did Joe Camper wear loud colorful socks?

He wanted to keep his feet from falling asleep.

What did Joe Camper call his black horse?
Night Mare.

Why did Joe Camper cut a hole in the carpet?
He wanted to see the floor show.

Why did Joe Camper eat a dollar?
It was his lunch money.

Why did Joe Camper give up waterskiing?
He couldn't find a lake with a hill in it.

Why did Joe Camper give cough syrup to the pony?
Someone told him the pony was a little horse.

Why did Joe Camper pitch his tent on the oven?
So he could have a home on the range.

What did Joe Camper call his pet zebra?
Spot.

Why did Joe Camper wear a wet T-shirt to bed?
The label said, "Wash and wear."

Why did Joe Camper bury the car battery?
Because it was dead.

Where was Joe Camper when the lights went out?
In the dark.

Why did Joe Camper take a ruler to bed?
He wanted to see how long he would sleep.

Why did Joe Camper reach for a bar of soap when his canoe overturned?
He thought he would wash up on shore.

Jester and Joe Camper

Joe Camper: Do you like my dog? It's a very rare breed. Part beagle and part bull. He cost me over two thousand dollars.
Jester: Really? Which part is bull?
Joe Camper: The part about the two thousand dollars.

Jester: We have a new dog too.
Joe Camper: What's he like?
Jester: Whatever we feed him.

Jester: Can you believe it. My dog doesn't even have a nose.
Joe Camper: How does he smell?
Jester: Terrible.

Jester: Did you know that there's a star called the Dog Star?
Joe Camper: Are you Sirius?

Joe Camper: Why does Joe Beagle wag his tail?
Jester: Because no one else will wag it for him.

Jester: Joe, your dog has been chasing a man on a bicycle.
Joe Camper: That's silly, my dog doesn't know how to ride a bike.

Joe Camper: Why is your dog staring at me while I'm eating?
Jester: He gets like that whenever someone eats from his plate.

Joe Camper: My dog's neck is always hanging down. I'm going to take him to the vet.
Jester: Neck's weak?
Joe Camper: No, tomorrow.

Teacher: Joe, your short story entitled "My Dog" reads exactly the same as your brother's.
Joe Camper: It's the same dog, sir.

Jester: Did I ever tell you about the time I came face to face with a mountain lion?
Joe Camper: No. What happened?
Jester: Well, I was totally unarmed. I stood my ground but he kept inching closer and closer toward me.
Joe Camper: What did you do?
Jester: Finally, I moved on to the next cage.

Jester: This match won't light.
Joe Camper: What's the matter with it?
Jester: I don't know, it worked a couple of minutes ago.

Jester: What's the difference between an elephant and a matterboy?
Joe Camper: What's a matterboy?
Jester: Nothing. What's a matter with you?

Jester: Did you hear about the latest sport to be having labor problems?
Joe Camper: No.

Jester: It seems professional bowlers have been talking strike.

Joe Camper: My shirt is always wrinkled, and my mom and I always fight about it.
Jester: I think you two should sit down and iron things out.

Jester: Did you hear the joke about the boy who fell on a bag of potato chips?
Joe Camper: No.
Jester: It's crummy.

Joe Camper: Mary, would you like to go out with me Saturday night?
Mary: I'm not really looking to get involved with one particular guy right now, Joe.
Joe Camper: Well lucky for you, I'm not known for being particular.

Joe Camper: My cabin on the boat was nice, but that washing machine on the wall was terrible?
Jester: That was no washing machine. That was the port hole.

Joe Camper: Well no wonder I didn't get any of my clothes back.

Jester: If I can prove that food is the mother of invention will you give me $10.00?
Joe Camper: OK.
Jester: Well food is a necessity, and an airplane is an invention and everyone knows that necessity is the mother of invention. Cough up the 10 bucks.

Jester: Do you want to see something swell?
Joe Camper: Sure.
Jester: Hit your head with a baseball bat.

Joe Camper: I'm always breaking into song.
Jester: You wouldn't have to if you could find the right key.

Jester: Joe, how much after midnight is it?
Joe Camper: I don't know. My watch only goes up to twelve.

Joe Beagle
The exciting adventures of Joe Camper's dog, Joe Beagle.

How did Joe Camper stop his dog, Joe Beagle, from barking in the back seat of his car?

> *He had Joe Beagle sit in the front.*

What happened when Joe Beagle chewed on a dictionary?

> *Joe Camper had to take the words right out of his mouth.*

What did Joe Beagle say when he sat on a piece of sandpaper?

> *Ruff-ruff.*

Why did Joe Beagle run in circles?

> *He was winding himself so that he could become a watchdog.*

What is Joe Beagle's favorite drink?
Pupsi Cola.

Why did Joe Beagle sit on the campfire?
He wanted to be a hot dog.

What happened to Joe Beagle after he ate garlic for a month?
His bark became worse than his bite.

What goes Krab, ffur, krab, ffur?
Joe beagle walking backwards.

Why did Joe Beagle have to pay a fine?
He got a barking ticket.

What does Joe Beagle do that Joe Camper steps into?
Pants

Is Joe Beagle a good watch dog?
Absolutely! If you hear a noise in the middle of the night and you wake him up, he'll bark like crazy.

Jester: Do you have a license for your dog, Joe Beagle?
Joe Camper: No, he's not old enough to drive.

Joe Camper: Jester, I'm so worried. I lost my dog.
Jester: Why don't you put an ad in the paper?
Joe Camper: It wouldn't help. My dog can't read.

Joe Camper: My dog is very smart.

Jester: Joe Beagle is absolutely the dumbest dog I've ever seen.

Joe Camper: That's not true. Joe Beagle is good at math.

Jester: Really?

Joe Camper: Absolutely. I once asked him how much is 10 minus 10. Sure enough, Joe Beagle said nothing.

Jester: Why is your dog running around in a circle like that?

Joe Camper: He thinks he's a watchdog, and he's winding himself.

Joe Camper: You look tired.

Jester: I ought to be. I was up all night chasing the dog in my pajamas.

Joe Camper: What was the dog doing in your pajamas?

The Trading Post

Camper: Do you carry tomato paste?
Trader Jack: Why do you have a broken tomato?

Camper: Toss me a box of that writing paper.
Trader Jack: I can't toss it if it's stationary.

Trader Jack: This is genuine Indian pottery.
Camper: But it says on the bottom made in Cleveland.
Trader Jack: Well haven't you ever heard of the Cleveland Indians?

Old Lady: Young man, I'd like to go to the trading post. Will you help me across the street?
Camper: Yes, but it would be easier if I helped you right here.
Old Lady: No, what I mean is, would you see me across the street?
Camper: Gee, I'm not sure. I'll run across and have a look.

91

Camper: How much do used batteries cost?
Trader Jack: Nothing they're free of charge.

Joe Camper: Hey, look! I bought this giant pack of cards at the trading post.
The Ranger: Big Deal.

It was a sweltering day, and Hermit the Frog was as hot as he could be. So he went to the trading post to see if his friend, Patty Wack, would let him have an ice cream cone. "Can I have some ice cream," Hermit asked as he walked to the window. "You know the rules," Patty responded, "what have you got to trade." Hermit searched his bag for something with which to barter. All he could find was a dusty Indian statue. "How about this?" Hermit croaked.

I'll have to ask Trader Jack," Patty
replied.

Patty explained the situation and
handed Trader Jack the statue. Then
she asked if she should accept the
statue in exchange for some ice
cream.

Trader Jack responded, "That's a
knick-knack, Patty Wack, give the
frog a cone."

A Camper sat in the trading post playing
checkers with Big Foot.

A stranger came in and stood
watching them play in complete
amazement.

When they finished their game he
came over and said, "I'm a television
reporter. You and your big hairy
friend here could make a fortune in
Washington, D.C."

The Camper just shrugged. "He's
not that clever," the Camper said
dismissively.

I've just beaten him two out of the
last three games."

A man walked into the snack bar at the trading post.

"Bring me a turtle sandwich," he demanded, "and make it snappy."

Two old college friends ran into each other at the trading post after many years apart.

The first man asked the second, "What have you been up to all these years."

The second man replied, "My life has been crazy. Believe it or not, I've been married four times. I married a millionaress first, then an actress, followed by a seamstress and then a mortician."

"That's a strange combination," said the first man. "Why did you marry them?"

"Well," the second man replied, "it was one for the money, two for the show, three to get ready and four to go."

Two Trout were dining at the trading post when one of them started to wave his empty canteen in the air.

The waiter turned to the busboy and said, "I think there's two fish out of water at table 5."

A customer went to the trading post and ordered a well-done steak. But when the waiter served it, the steak was very rare.

Angry, the customer called out, "Didn't you hear me say, 'well done?'"

"No, but thank you," replied the waiter. "I don't get many compliments."

A boy was brought to court for stealing a backpack from the trading post. He told the judge that it wasn't his intention to keep the backpack; he had just taken it as a joke to see if it would be missed.

"Since you took it all the way home," the judge answered, "I'm going to give you 30 days for carrying a joke too far."

Two eggs, an English muffin and 3 sausages walk into the trading post. "Let me have a soda for each of my friends," says one of the eggs.

I'm sorry," Trader Jack replied. "We don't serve breakfast."

Camper versus Leader

Leader: Each of you needs to eat all of your vegetables. There are thousands of starving children who would love to have them.
Camper: Name two.

Leader: Why do you always have to answer my questions with another question?
Camper: Why not?

Camper: If I'm good throughout the entire camping trip, will you give me a dollar?
Leader: Absolutely not! When I was your age I was good for nothing.

Camper: What causes the holes in those boards?
Leader: Those are knot holes.
Camper: If they're not holes, what are they?

Leader: Do any of you boys know who homer was?

Camper: Yeah, he was the guy Babe Ruth made famous.

Leader: Can you telephone from a submarine?
Camper: Of course, everyone can tell a phone from a submarine.

Leader: What made you go out on that unsafe ice and risk your life to save your friend?
Camper: I had to do it; he was wearing my skates.

Leader: Why are you guys returning so late from the orienteering course?
Camper: We were following this Tates compass, but it kept sending us in circles.
Leader: You idiots. Don't you know he who has a Tates is lost!

Camper: I'm too tired to wash the dishes.
Leader: Nonsense, a little hard work never killed anyone.
Camper: Then why should I run the risk of being the first?

Leader: Why are you carrying only one log for the campfire, when all the other kids have their hands completely full?
Camper: I guess the other kids are too lazy to make more than one trip.

Leader: The only way to acquire a new skill is to start at the bottom.
Camper: But I want to learn to swim.

Leader: When I was young my parents told me if I made ugly faces my face would stay that way forever.
Camper: Well, you can't say you weren't warned.
Camper: At summer camp we slept in 20 foot long beds.
Leader: That sounds like a lot of bunk to me.
Camper: Can someone tell me anything about soldiers from the Revolutionary War?
Leader: They're all dead.

Leader: How did you get that black eye?
Camper: Sir, I was hit by a guided muscle with a knucklear warhead!

Leader: To complete your bird study you must name these three birds.
Camper: This is easy. I'll name them Harold, Irving and Polly.

Leader: I lost my toupee this morning.
Camper: I think we should comb the area.

More with Jester and Joe Camper

Joe Camper: Do you want to hear me sing the camp song?
Jester: Only if it's solo.
Joe Camper: What do you mean?
Jester: Only if it's so low I can't hear it.

Jester: Did you hear about my pinewood derby car?
Joe Camper: No.
Jester: It was a wooden car with wooden wheels and a wooden engine. The only problem I had was it wooden go.

Jester: Lend me 50 cents.
Joe Camper: I only have forty.
Jester: In that case, give me 40. You can owe me a dime.

Joe Camper: I'd like to go on a date with a girl who's the exact opposite of me.
Jester: No problem Joe, there are a lot of bright girls around.

Joe Camper: Hey Jester, what are you doing?
Jester: Writing a letter to my little sister.
Joe Camper: How come you're writing it so slowly?
Jester: Because she can't read very fast.

Jester: Hey Joe, how old would a person be who was born in 1950?
Joe Camper: Man or woman?

Jester: Joe, I heard you singing this morning.
Joe Camper: Yeah, I was just killing time.
Jester: Looks like you had an effective weapon.

Jester: I had a terrible nightmare last night, Joe. I dreamt I was a salad.
Joe Camper: What's terrible about that?

Jester: I tossed all night.

Jester: My doctor says I need to work out with dumbbells.
Joe Camper: Why are you telling me?
Jester: Well, I was wondering if you wanted to go jogging.

Jester: I had a fight with my brother last night.
When it was over he crawled to me on his hands and knees.

Joe Camper: What did he say?
Jester: Come out from under the bed.
Joe Camper: A pirate?
Jester: Yeah, murder on the high C's.

Joe Camper: I wish I had enough money to buy a walrus.

Jester: A walrus? What do you want a walrus for?

Joe Camper: I don't. I just want the money.

Joe Camper: I heard a joke the other day, I wonder if I told it to you?

Jester: Was it funny?

Joe Camper: Yes.

Jester: Then you haven't.

Joe Camper: What do you do if you are attacked by a Wild Adirondack Cow?

Jester: Use the buddy system.
Joe Camper: The buddy system?
Jester: Yeah, when a WAC attacks, push your buddy toward it.

Jester: If you can guess how many candy bars I have I'll give you both of them.
Joe Camper: Hmmmm.....I'll say three.

Jester: I made an upside down cake on an open campfire last week.
Joe Camper: How'd it turn out?
Jester: Actually, it was a complete flop.

Joe Camper: Listen to me. I sing like a bird.
Jester: No, you sound more like a pirate to me.

Joe Camper: I've eaten beef all my life and now I'm strong as a bull.
Jester: That's funny, I've eaten fish all my life and I can't swim a stroke.

Joe Camper: The two things I cook best are meatloaf and upside down cake.

Jester: Which one is this?

Joe Camper: A bee stung me!!!
Jester: Try putting some ointment on it.
Joe Camper: But the bee's probably miles away by now.

Jester: I tied a piece of yellow string around my finger to keep lions away while we're at camp.
Joe Camper: There are no lions here.
Jester: Good, the string seems to be working.

Jester: Don't open my trunk. It contains a 10 foot snake.
Joe Camper: You can't fool me. Even I know snakes don't have 10 feet.

Joe Camper: I crashed my bicycle. I went out for a ride, and I hit a cow.
Jester: A jersey cow?
Joe Camper: I don't know. I didn't see the license plate.

Hermit the Frog Jokes

What is Hermit the Frog's favorite flower?
A crocus.

Who is green and lives alone in the woods?
Hermit the Frog.

What famous Pole is related to Hermit the Frog?
Tad Pole.

What does Hermit the Frog drink?
Croak-a-cola.

What is Hermit the Frog's favorite game?
Croquet

What happened to Hermit the Frog when he sat in the no parking area?

He got toad away.

How did Hermit the Frog die?

He croaked.

Why couldn't Hermit the Frog speak?

He had a person in his throat.

What did Hermit the Frog become when he broke his leg?

Unhoppy.

Where does Hermit the Frog hang his jacket?

In the croak room.

What kind of shoes does Hermit the Frog like?

Open toad shoes.

What game does his Scottish cousin like?

Hop Scotch.

Why did Hermit the Frog yell at the waiter?

There was no fly in his soup.

Why is Hermit the Frog happy?
He gets to eat what bugs him.

How does Hermit the Frog start his car when it won't turn over?
Jump start.

What did Hermit the Frog eat with his hamburger when he was in Paris?
French Flies.

What's evergreen, grows in the spring, and hops around?
A tree frog.

Jokes

An American Camper troop was visiting Russia. Their guide's name was Rudolph, a staunch red communist, and throughout the trip, the Leader and Rudolph argued about everything starting with their differing political views. As the troop was getting ready to leave, the Leader said, "Look, it's starting to snow."

> The guide immediately disagreed, "No, sir, it's raining out."
> "I still think it's snowing," said the Leader.
> The Leader's wife, weary of all this bickering interrupted the battle.
> "I think Rudolph the Red knows rain dear."

A leader decided to use some psychology to try to get his lazy campers to do some work. So he said, "I've got a nice easy job for the laziest Camper here. Any volunteers?"

> In an instant all but one of the Campers raised their hands. "Why didn't you raise your hand," the Leader asked him?
> "Too much work," he replied.

A deer and an antelope were wandering through camp late one night. Suddenly, the antelope stopped and cocked his head. "What's the matter," asked the deer.

> The antelope answered, "I thought I just heard a discouraging word."

A Leader was sick and tired of constantly answering ridiculous questions from the new Campers. So finally, he instituted a rule, that anyone who asked a question that he himself couldn't answer, would have to wash everyone else's mess kit after supper.

> This didn't stop Jester who asked more questions than anyone else. He

asked, "When a chipmunk digs its hole, how come it doesn't leave a pile of dirt around the entrance?"

"Answer it yourself," the campers chimed gleefully.

"A chipmunk starts digging its hole from the inside," Jester explained. The Leader looked at him incredulously, and asked, "How could he get to the inside to start digging?"

"You made the rule," Jester answered, "you answer or start washing."

A group of Campers sat down for dinner at summer camp. One of the new boys was about to ask someone to pass him the bread, when one of the Campers stood up and yelled "63" and everyone in the room laughed. Another Camper called out "29" and the whole room went into hysterics. The new Camper was confused so he asked one of the older campers to explain what was going on.

"Well you see," he responded, "we've been coming to camp so long that we already know all the jokes. So we listed them with numbers on a piece of paper; now, instead of retelling a joke, we just yell out the number; everyone knows which joke it is, and they laugh."

The new Camper thinks the whole idea is clever and he decides to give it a try. So he stands up and yells, "Fourteen," and the entire room gets quiet.

"What did I do wrong," the new camper asked when nobody laughed.

"Oh nothing," replied the older camper, "It's just that some people know how to tell a joke, and some people don't."

The highlight of camp Maine's annual winter campout was the ice fishing competition. Each patrol drilled their holes in the ice and began fishing. After several minutes the panther campsite was reeling in one fish after another, while the other campsites continued to have no luck. A young camper approached the campsite Leader to ask what he was doing wrong.

"Ymm umm wmm umm," the Patrol Leader replied.

"What?" asked the boy again.

"Ymm umm wmm umm," he said again.

"What?"

Finally, the Patrol Leader spit a bunch of worms into his hand and said, "You have to keep the worms warm."

The world's smartest man, the Pope, and a Boy Scout were on a transcontinental flight. Suddenly, the pilot burst into the cabin. The plane is going to crash. Grab a parachute and jump. With that he took one of the three parachutes and jumped out of the plane. The world's smartest man said to the Pope and the Boy Scout. "I'm on the verge of developing a cure for cancer. I have a plan for world peace. I'm too important to die." He reached into the closet, slipped his arms into the straps and jumped.

> The Pope turned to the Boy Scout and said, "I've lived a long life my son. You take the final parachute."
> "Don't worry your holiness," the Boy Scout said. "There are still two parachutes left. When the world's smartest man jumped, he took my backpack."

Two Campers were walking through the woods when suddenly a mountain lion leaped out in front of them. The first Camper cautioned the second to remain calm. "Remember what we read in the Handbook. If you stand absolutely still, and look the lion straight in the eye, he will turn and run away."

> The second Camper said, "Fine, you've read the handbook, and I've read the handbook, but has the lion read the handbook?"

When the campers visited the zoo, the zookeeper was very upset because the gnu's had separated into two groups. One group was always fighting while the other group always got along.

He wanted to get rid of the group that fought because there's no gnu's like good gnu's.

A flashlight was charged with assault and battery.

At the hearing the judge said,

"I'm reducing your charge to simple assault, because in your case, batteries are Not included."

After annoying campers with difficult first aid questions while teaching them proper first aid, and yelling when questions were answered wrong, leader turned the meeting over to his assistant. The assistant reviewed first aid again to prepare the patrol for when the leader came back for another test. Completing a lengthy discussion on tourniquets, the assistant asked, "What would you do if the Leader received a serious head wound?"

"Put a tourniquet around his neck," the patrol replied in unison.

During a visit to the local zoo, a Camper spent nearly an hour trying to awaken a bear. He had hoped to take a picture of the bear in action so that could tell fellow Campers he had confronted this animal in the wild. When the zookeeper came over the Camper impatiently asked, "What kind of bear is that anyway?"

"Himalayan," the zookeeper replied. "I know that," screamed the camper. "I want to know when him a gettin up."

After a week of bad rain, the camp was filled with a variety of insects. All day long mosquitoes bothered the campers, and at night the sky was filled with fireflies.

When one of the younger Campers saw the fireflies, he turned to his nearby friend and said, "I think we'd better go inside the tent. They're looking for us with flashlights now."

On a dock one day, two boys were preparing to get into a boat.

"Can I go downstairs?" one of the younger boys inquired.

"Let's get something straight," the older boy responded, "Downstairs is below deck. Right is starboard. Left is port. The front is the bow and the back is the stern. You need to start using the correct terminology. One more mistake like "downstairs" and I'll throw you out one of those little round windows."

Let's get our bearings straight. Directly in front of us is due north. To our right is east, and west is to the left. Now let's see if you guys can figure this out. What's at our backs?

"Knapsacks," the boys replied.

Lester Rope stops into town to check out the local watering hole.

"Let me have a root beer please," the rope says to the restaurant owner. The owner promptly picks up Lester Rope and throws him outside. "We don't serve rope here. Get out and stay out."

The rope moves on to another tavern and has the same experience. Feeling dejected, Lester makes plans to leave town, when another rope approaches him and says, "Hey, what's the matter man, how come you're so down in the dumps?"

Lester Rope replies, "Nobody in this town likes me. I can't even get a restaurant to serve me."

The second rope laughs, "You're going about this all wrong. You need to be hip to get served in a happening town like this."

So the second rope instructs Lester to tie himself into a square knot. He then says, "To be really punk,

you need to frazzle your hair."
So Lester Rope complies,
separating his strands to give him
the appearance of a punk hair do.
With that, he and his new friend go
in search of a good time.
"Don't go in there," Lester warns, as
they approach one of the restaurants
which had earlier refused to serve
him. "Don't worry," says the punk
rope, "just follow my lead."
So the punk rope steps up to the
counter and orders a couple of sodas.
The waiter returns and serves them.
Eyeing the pair suspiciously, the
waiter says, "Hey - wait a minute -
are you a rope?"
And the rope replies, "Afrayed
knot."

There was a Camper named Joe Bajerkolopouliskowski who always hated his name. So he waited and waited for his 18th birthday, and when it arrived, he went down to the courthouse to have his name legally changed.

The clerk asked, "What do you choose as your new name?"

"Lester Bajerkolopouliskowski," he replied.

Camp Inuit challenged camp Miwok to a football game. The teams were well matched and the score was tied 0-0 as Inuit hiked the ball with just a few minutes left on the clock. Just as the ball was snapped, a train went whirling past the field blowing its horn. The boys from Miwok mistook the horn for the signal that time had expired, so they walked off the field.

Three plays later, the boys from Camp Inuit scored the winning touchdown.

Did you hear the one about the hermit who got into trouble for driving into town?

He was charged with recluse driving.

A Leader was watching a new Camper on his first campout. The Camper reached into his pack and pulled out his dinner; a meal which consisted of a bag of chips, a candy bar, a bottle of soda, and a can of pudding.

"Don't you know the four basic food groups?" the Leader asked the new Camper.

"Certainly," the boy replied.

"Bagged, wrapped, bottled and canned."

Did you hear about the Leader who threatened to kill his Campers if they didn't collect the morning mist in a bottle?

It was a case of dew or die.

On the first day at camp, the Leader called together the entire camp. "OK," he asked, "who pushed the outhouse into the river?" No one admitted to doing it. So the Leader said, "I want to tell you a story about

George Washington. When he was a boy he cut down his father's favorite cherry tree. His father asked him if he did it, and when he told the truth, he didn't get into any trouble because he was honest."

"Now we all know good campers are honest," the Leader stated. So I'm going ask again, "Who pushed the outhouse into the river?"
The Leader's son answered, "Father, I cannot tell a lie. I pushed the outhouse in the river."
The Leader started chasing after his son and screaming at him.
"But dad," the boy cried, "what about George Washington?"
The Leader responded, "George Washington's father wasn't in the cherry tree."

Two Campers were walking through the woods when suddenly they stumbled upon a large black bear. Immediately, one of the two removed his hiking boots, reached into his pack and slipped on a pair of running shoes. "What are you doing?" his companion asked incredulously. "You know that you can't outrun a bear, even with those on."

"Who cares about the bear," the first hiker replied. "All I need to worry about is outrunning you."

A young Camper was interested in learning first aid. While teaching him, the Leader asked what items should be included in a first aid kit. The Camper listed many items including a jar of mayonnaise.

"Why would you put a jar of mayonnaise in a first aid kit?" the Leader inquired.

"Because," the young Camper replied, The book says to 'include a dressing.'"

Joe Camper was bragging about the 25-pound trout he had caught while ice fishing. "Twenty-five pounds," the Leader replied skeptically, "Were there any witnesses?"

"Of course," Joe Camper replied. "Otherwise it would have been a fifty pounder."

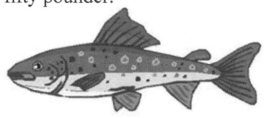

Joe Camper was telling his fellow Campers how getting trained in first aid had prepared him for an emergency. "I saw a women hit by a truck," he stated. "She had a twisted ankle, broken bones, and a fractured skull."

"How terrible! What did you do?"
"Thanks to my first-aid training, I knew just how to handle it. I sat on the ground, and put my head between my knees to keep from fainting."

A Camper fell down a very deep crevasse, breaking both arms. A quick thinking friend lowered down a rope and instructed the Camper to bite hard onto the rope. Inch by inch, members of the campsite gingerly pulled the Camper toward the top of the crevasse, while he bit firmly on the rope. As he reached the top, the leader called out.

"Are you O.K.?"

"Yes, AAAAAAAAAAAAAAAAAAHHHHHHHHHH!!!!" he replied.

Joe Camper visited Toronto with plans to try his hand at ice fishing. He pitched his tent and got ready to cut a hole in the ice. As he pulled the cord on his chain saw, he heard a voice from above, "There are no fish under the ice."

He pulled the cord again, and the same voice emanated from above, "There are no fish under the ice." Awestruck, Joe Camper looked reverently at the heavens. "Is that you God," he inquired.

"No," the voice replied. "I own this rink, and I can tell you, there are no fish under the ice."

Joe Camper walked down the street carrying a computer and a desk. A police officer walked up to him and said, "I'm afraid I'm going to have to place you under arrest."

"But wait officer," Joe Camper replied, "these items aren't stolen, they belong to me."

"Oh, I realize those items aren't stolen."

"Then what's the charge?" Joe Camper queried "Impersonating an office, sir."

A women lion tamer had the vicious animals under such complete control that she could command them to take a lump of sugar from her lips and they would obey. Joe Camper stood skeptically by the cage and yelled, "Anyone could do that."

The ringmaster came over and asked, "Would you like to try?"

"Sure," replied Joe Camper. "But first, get those crazy lions out of there!"

Joe Camper decided to take up painting so he went to the store to buy an easel.
At the art supply store they carried two sizes small and large.
Joe thought about it for a moment and decided to choose the lesser of two easels.

Joe Camper was trying to light a match. He struck one, but it wouldn't light. He struck a second, but it didn't burn either. Finally, he struck a third match and it lit right up.
"That's a good one," Joe proclaimed as he blew out the match. "I'll have to save it."

Joe Camper got careless with matches and lit the field behind his house on fire. Thinking quickly, he ran into the house and called the fire department.
"The field is on fire,"
Joe Camper cried into the phone.

"Calm down," the dispatcher intoned. "Now how do we get to the field?"

"Don't you still have that red truck?" Joe inquired.

Two Campers accompanied Joe Camper for a hike across the desert. The first camper carried a canteen of water; the second camper brought along a loaf of bread. Joe Camper was carrying a car door. A prospector came upon the trio and struck up a conversation. He said to the first camper, "Why do you have that there canteen of water with you?" "Because there's not much water out here," the first Camper replied.

He turned to the second and asked, "How come you're carrying that there loaf of bread?" The second

Camper answered, "So I have something to eat when I get hungry." The prospector then started scratching his head as he turned to address Joe Camper. "Why are you a carryin' that there car door?" "Well," replied Joe Camper, "so I can roll down the window when it gets hot."

After breaking his arm, Joe Camper asked the doctor. "Will I be able to play the violin when the cast comes off?" "Of course you will," replied the doctor.

"That's great," stammered Joe. "I always wished I could play the violin."

Joe Camper visited a farm for the first time. "I've been watching that bull over there for some time," Joe Camper related, "and I don't understand how come he doesn't have any horns?"

"Well," replied the farmer, "sometimes we saw off the horns when they're young so the bulls don't poke us. The horns sometimes fall off the older bulls. As for that bull there, the reason why he doesn't have any horns is because he's a horse."

Joe Camper handed his teacher a drawing featuring an airplane covered with grapes, apples, bananas and oranges. Puzzled, the teacher turned to Joe and said, "The theme for today's drawings was supposed to be related to patriotic American songs. How is that drawing related to our topic?"
"You know the song America the Beautiful," Joe Camper replied. "Well that's the fruited plane."

Joe Camper took his little cousin with him when he went fishing. When he got back to the campsite, he was extremely fed up.
"I'm never taking him with me again," Joe complained.
"Did he scare away the fish," the ranger wondered.

"No," muttered Joe Camper. "He sat on the bank all day eating my earthworms."

Joe Camper ran into the emergency room, jumped on top of the doctor and started yelling, "One, two, three, four."
"What's going on here!" the doctor yelled while struggling to free himself.
"Well, doctor," Joe Camper replied. "They told me in admissions that I could count on you."

When Joe Camper first went to camp, a group of boys convinced him to try his hand at elephant hunting. Several hours after he started, he returned to camp empty-handed.
"You didn't catch anything, did ya?" one of the boys asked Joe Camper.
"No, I gave up because the decoys got too heavy," Joe Camper replied.

Once again, the SPL was giving the Albino Polar Bear Patrol a first aid test. Turning to Joe Camper the SPL asked, "What would you do if your sister swallowed the key to your house?"

"I'd climb in through the window," Joe Camper replied.

Joe Camper ordered a large pizza. The cook pulled the pizza out of the oven and asked Joe Camper, "Do you want me to cut it into 6 or 8 pieces?"

"Better make it six," Joe Camper responded, "I could never eat eight pieces."

Joe Camper came back to the campsite after a long day of hiking. "My stomach hurts," he complained. "That must be because your stomach is empty," the Leader reasoned. "You'd feel much better if you had something in it." Later that night the Leader complained that he was suffering from a terrible headache. "That must be because your head is empty," Joe Camper reasoned. "You'd feel much better if you had something in it."

A psychiatrist was questioning Joe Camper. "Do you ever hear voices without being able to tell who is speaking, or where the voices are coming from?" he asked.

"All the time," Joe replied.
"And when does this occur?" asked the doctor.
"When I answer the phone."

Joe Camper went into the trading post and ordered a gallon of chocolate ice cream. "I'm sorry," replied Trader Jack, "We're all out of Chocolate."

"All right then," Joe replied. "I'll have a pint of chocolate."

"Joe," Trader Jack intoned. "We have strawberry and we have vanilla, but we have no chocolate."

"Well, I'll just have a small chocolate cone then," Joe replied.

"Joe, pay close attention." Trader Jack said. "Can you spell the *van* in vanilla?"

"Sure," Joe replied, "That's easy V-A-N."

"And can you spell the *straw* in strawberry?"

"Certainly," Joe answered. "S-T-R-A-W."

"And how about the *cottonpick* in chocolate?"

"There's no *cottonpick* in chocolate," Joe said.

"Exactly!"

"Do you really sell that many jackknifes?" Joe Camper asked Trader Jack, as the boy examined shelf after shelf lined with jackknifes.

"No," Trader Jack responded. "I maybe sell one or two a month. The truth is I'm not a very good knife seller. But the guy who sells me jackknifes; now he's a good Knife seller."

Joe Camper took out the gas can and began to refill his lawn mower. As usual, he was not paying much attention to what he was doing. He overfilled the tank, and gasoline formed a pool alongside the mower. Sadly, Joe Beagle, Joe Camper's faithful dog, ran over and lapped up the gasoline. Joe Camper tried to stop the dog, but the beagle ran in a crazed frenzy around the yard. For twenty minutes Joe Camper chased after the dog when suddenly the dog coughed, stopped and passed out on the lawn.

A concerned neighbor rushed over and asked, "What's the matter with your dog?"
"He ran out of gas," Joe Camper replied.

"I'm really worried about Joe Beagle," Joe Camper said to the veterinarian. "I dropped some coins on the floor, and before I could pick them up, he ate them." The veterinarian told Joe he would need to leave his dog at the office overnight for observation.

The next morning Joe Camper called to see how his dog was doing. The vet replied, "no change yet."

Joe Beagle visited an old western saloon and ordered a drink. The bartender sneered, grabbed his gun and shot Joe Beagle in the foot. "Scram," he snarled, "we don't serve dogs here."

A week later Joe Beagle returned with a bandaged leg and a six shooter. A new man was tending bar. Limping up to the bar, Joe Beagle said, "I'm looking for the man who shot my paw."

Joe Camper and Joe Beagle walked into a restaurant. They were stopped at the door by a waiter who said, "I'm sorry, no dogs allowed." "But wait," responded Joe, "this is a talking dog. I'll ask him three questions, and if he answers them correctly, promise you'll let us stay." The waiter agreed.

Joe asked his dog, "What's the opposite of smooth?"

"R-r-ruff," barked his dog.

"What's on top of a house?"

"R-r-roof", the Beagle responded.

"Right again," cried Joe Camper. "Now who's the best baseball player?"

"R-r-ruth," said the dog.

The waiter then threw Joe Camper and Joe Beagle into the alley saying, "Don't ever come back in here again."

As they lay there, Joe Beagle looked quizzically at Joe Camper and said, "Aaron?"

While staying at Camp, Joe Camper and Joe Beagle decided to try some fishing. While grabbing a boat Joe asked the ranger how the fishing was.

"Fishing's great," he replied.

After several hours on the water, Joe Camper hadn't caught a fish. Disgusted he returned the boat to the ranger. "I thought you said the fishing was great," Joe Camper stammered.

"The fishing's always great," replied the ranger, "catchin 'em is what's difficult."

Joe Camper and Joe Beagle went hiking and wandered onto some private property. A recluse and his wife encountered the duo and the man began yelling at Joe Camper for trespassing. With that Joe Beagle went over and bit the stranger, then cornered the stranger's wife and did the same.

"I can understand why your dog bit me," the recluse cried. "But why did he have to go off and bite my poor wife."

"To get the bad taste out of his mouth," Joe Camper replied.

A businessman placed a classified ad for a position he had open. The job required a bilingual person who could type, take dictation, and operate a computer.

The first to apply for the position was a dog named Joe Beagle. Not wanting to discriminate, the business owner gave the dog the standard secretarial test. To his surprise, the dog was a wizard with the computer; he took dictation well, and typed nearly 150 words per minute.

"I'm very impressed with your qualifications," the businessman told the dog. "But there is still one requirement. Are you bilingual?"

Joe Beagle barked, wagged his tail, and then answered the question. "Meow," he replied.

A woman was eating her lunch by the lake. Joe Camper and his faithful dog Joe Beagle were sitting nearby. Joe Beagle smelled the woman's food and began to whine.

> "You don't mind if I throw him a bit, do you?" the women inquired.
> "Not at all," Joe Camper replied.
> So the women picked Joe Beagle up and threw him in the lake.

Joe Camper and Jester decided to stop for dinner at an area steak house. Jester ordered a porterhouse steak, Joe Camper asked for a lobster tail. After about 10 minutes the waitress returned with a steak in one hand and a book in the other. She gave the steak to Jester, and then she opened the book and sat down next to Joe Camper.

> "Once upon a time", she began, "there was a little lobster."

Joe Camper took his dog Joe Beagle with him to see the movie, *101 Dalmatians*. When the usher noticed the dog he was about to throw him out, but relented when he saw that the animal seemed to be paying very close attention to the film. After the show, the usher went over to Joe Camper. "It certainly surprised me to see your dog enjoying this film, he said.

"It surprised me too," Joe Camper replied. "He didn't like the book at all."

Joe and Jester were hiking through the forest. Suddenly the Jester stopped short and took a deep sigh.

"What's wrong," Joe Camper queried?
"Nothing," Jester replied. "But I sure wish Miss Manners was with us."
"Why?" Joe Camper asked.
"Because I think we took the wrong fork."

Joe and Jester were standing over a dead man named Juan. "I think he was killed with a golf gun," Jester surmised.

"A golf gun?" wondered Joe Camper. "What's a golf gun?"
"I don't know, but it sure made a hole in Juan."

Jester and Joe Camper grabbed a canoe and decided to go fishing. After a very successful day Jester said, "We really should mark this spot so we can come back tomorrow." So Joe Camper painted an "X" on the bottom of the boat.

"You idiot," Jester jeered. "That's not very smart. What happens if we come back tomorrow and they give us a different boat?"

Joe Camper and Jester were tracking a bear along the Appalachian Trail.

After some time the tracks disappeared.
They decided to continue on in hopes of picking up bear tracks again.

After walking a little further along the trail they came to a fork in the path.
A sign advised them, bear left.
So they decided to go home too.

Joe and Jester bought two horses from a local farm.

The horses were very similar, and the two friends could never tell them apart.
So they shaved the mane off one horse, but it grew back.
They then cut the tail off the other horse, but it also grew back.
Exasperated, Joe finally got the clever idea of measuring the height of each horse, because it appeared one horse might be slightly bigger than the other.
Sure enough, their problem was solved once and for all.
It turns out that the white horse is a quarter of an inch taller than the black one.

Jester walked into a fish market and asked the owner to toss him the biggest fish he had.

"Why do you want me to throw it to you?" the owner asked.

Jester responded, "So when I go home I can honestly say that I caught it."

Joe Camper and Jester were talking about cooking. "I got me a cookbook once," Joe Camper claimed, "but I never could do a thing with it."

"Too many fancy dishes?" Jester inquired.

"Yup," every one of them started out the same way. "Take a clean dish...and that ended my cooking right there."

Joe Camper and Jester stood by the Leader's car. Foolishly, Joe Camper had locked the leader's keys in the car.

"Why don't we get a coat hanger to open it," Jester inquired.

"Where are we going to find a coat hanger in the middle of the woods?" Joe responded.

"Well what if we just cut the rubber with my pocket knife. Then we could stick our finger down and pull up the lock."

"The Leader would kill us if we wrecked his window like that."

"Well, we better think of something," Jester replied with a sigh. "It's starting to rain and the sun roof is wide open."

Joe Camper and Jester decided to try their hand at tracking animals. After hiking around for a while, they uncovered their first set of tracks. "Them are bear tracks," Joe Camper informed Jester.

"Don't be ridiculous," Jester replied. "Those are obviously deer tracks." So the two stood there arguing for several hours, until a train nearly hit them.

Joe was telling Jester about his trip to the Rockies. Jester asked, "What did you think of the scenery?"

"Oh, I couldn't really see much," Joe explained, "There were too many mountains in the way."

At the campfire, Joe Camper announced that he was going to sing one of his favorite tunes, "Over the river and far away."

"Thank goodness," whispered Jester. "I thought he was going to stay here singing all night."

During a rainy day at camp Joe Camper began working on a 200-piece jigsaw puzzle. After working on it every night for 2 weeks, the puzzle was finally finished. "Looky what I've done, Jester," Joe Camper shrieked excitedly to his friend.

"That's pretty good, Joe. How long did it take you to do that?"

"Only two weeks," Joe proudly replied.

"Is two weeks fast?" Jester inquired.

"You bet," Joe Camper exclaimed. "Look at the box. It says, from 2 to 4 years."

Jester was ironing his Camper uniform while Joe Camper entertained himself watching TV. "I'm going to get a soda," Jester said as he left Joe Camper alone in the living room. When he returned he was surprised to find that Joe Camper had a serious burn on both ears. "What happened?" Jester asked as he glanced at his injured friend.

> "Well, I was watching TV when the phone rang. I absentmindedly picked up the iron, and placed it to my ear."
> "That's terrible," Jester replied.
> "How did you burn the other ear?"
> "They called back."

Joe Camper and Jester were contemplating sneaking out of camp after dark. When no one was aware, Joe Camper slipped away from the campsite to determine if there was a good place to climb over the fence, or to tunnel under it. Joe Camper returned with a disappointed look on his face. "We can't tunnel under, or climb over the fence. I guess we can't leave the camp," he complained.

"Why not," Jester asked.

"Because there's no fence."

At the campfire, Joe Camper volunteered to play his trumpet. The noise was awful. After finishing his first song, Joe asked the group, "Is there anything you would like me to play?"

"Yes," cried Jester. "How about playing dominoes?"

Joe Camper and Jester were out in their boat one day when a hand appeared in the ocean.

"What's that?" Joe Camper wondered. "It looks as if someone is drowning."

"Nonsense," replied Jester. "It was just a little wave."

Joe Camper decided to enroll in truck driving school. At the end of a long day of class the instructor began quizzing Joe Camper on what he had learned. "You're in an eighteen wheeler," the instructor began, "carrying a heavy load barreling down a two lane highway. Jester, your co-driver is asleep. There are eight trucks behind you, and as you come over the top of a hill, they pull out beside you to pass. Suddenly you see several trucks coming in the opposite direction pulling into your lane to pass. What do you do?"

"That's simple," Joe Camper replied. "I'd wake up Jester."

"Why would you do that?" asked the instructor.

"Because," replied Joe Camper, "Jester ain't never seen a truck wreck like this before!"

It Isn't Easy Being a Leader

The Leader always believed that five was his lucky number. He was born on May 5, 1955. He had 5 children. He lived at 555 West 55th street. On his 55th birthday he went to the track, and he was surprised to find a horse named Numero Cinco running in the fifth race. So 5 minutes before the race, he went to the fifth window and put down $5,555 on Numero Cinco.

Sure enough, the horse finished fifth.

On the first day of the national Jamboree, Leaders from all over the country gathered for a cracker barrel. A Leader from Massachusetts spent the whole evening listening to a Leader from Texas brag about the heroes of the Alamo. Finally, the

Texan said, "I'll bet you never had anyone that brave in Boston."

> "Haven't you ever heard of Paul Revere?" asked the Bostonian.
> "Paul Revere?" said the Texan. "Oh, yeah; wasn't he the guy who ran for help?"

A Leader was racing along Interstate 95 at ninety-five miles an hour when he was pulled over by a state trooper. "Why were you going so fast," the trooper inquired?

> "Well," the Leader replied, "I saw the sign back there that said 95 and I was just doing the speed limit."
> "Well," the trooper sighed. "It's a good thing I caught you before you got to Interstate 395."

A Leader saw a group of young Campers gathered around a small cat. "What are you boys up to," the Leader inquired.

> "Trading lies," one of the Campers replied. "We found this cat and whoever can tell the biggest lie will get to keep the kitten."

"Why when I was your age, I would never think of telling lies," the Leader said incredulously.
"Okay, you win," the campers unanimously cried. "The cats yours."

The Leader asked each patrol to put together a list of who, in their opinion, were the 9 greatest Americans of Today. After about 20 minutes the Leader visited the Panther Patrol. "Have you finished your list yet?" he wondered.
"No, not yet. We still can't decide on a center fielder."

The Leader noticed that Joe Camper had been daydreaming through the entire first aid training session. He decided to try and get Joe's full attention. "Joe," he said, "If a fire truck is red, and first aid kits are 2 for ten dollars, how old am I?"
"Thirty-four," Joe answered without hesitation.
"That's amazing," the Leader responded. "How did you ever guess?"

"That's easy," Joe replied. "My older brother is seventeen and he's only half crazy."

A Leader walked into a train station and requested a ticket to the moon.

"I'm sorry," the agent reported, "but the moon is full."

"That's wonderful keeping a lion and a monkey in the same cage," said the Leader who was visiting a small zoo. "How do they get along?"

"Okay usually," answered the zookeeper. "Occasionally they have a disagreement and we need to get a new monkey."